VINTAGE MAPS

Awash with beautiful colors and rich details, the Old World charm of this elegant antique map artwork is embellished with luxurious foil accents and offers a glimpse into the artistic expression of geography and celestial objects in the ancient world.

Cover Art:
The Situation of the Earth in the Heavens, plate 74 from 'The Celestial Atlas, or the Harmony of the Universe' (Atlas coelestis seu harmonia macrocosmica) pub. by Joannes Janssonius, Amsterdam, 1660-1 (engraving), Cellarius, Andreas (c.1596-1665) (after) / Private Collection / Bridgeman Images

Published by teNeues Publishing Company
©teNeues Publishing Company
All rights reserved.
www.teneues.nyc

teNeues
www.teneues.com